"What are we going to do now

By

Rod Wheelwright

This book is dedicated to my beautiful lovely three daughters Heather, Abbey, and Lucy, who helped keep me sane during lockdown.

Without their help, I don't know how I would have coped. Regardless of what anyone says about this pandemic, it is the children who will be affected by this and they will be able to tell their stories in the future of how they managed to get through it.

I hope when my children are older, they can go over to a bookshelf, dust down this book, and tell their children of the fun times we had making things and keeping ourselves occupied when the shops were shut.

My children's faces have been covered up in this book to protect their identity. My face has not been so please don't think their father was Mr smiley face.

I would just like to add a thank you to Pets at Home for letting me use all the cardboard that was waiting to be recycled but instead made to make priceless memories. I have also included posts from my Facebook page. These posts show what we were doing during lockdown. However, my spelling and punctuation aren't brilliant, and I apologise for that.

Thank God and Zuckerberg we didn't delete them.

Enjoy

Rod

Chapter One

Chitty Chitty Bang Clang!!!

Rod Wheelwright

9 Mar 2020 · 👥

• • •

So I got this empty cardboard box from work and said to the girls today before they went to playgroup/school that I was going to make a puppet theatre with it as Lucy wanted. Straight away Heather says daddy why don't you make a chitty chitty bang bang car with it.

Oh I   I have my work cut out.

P.s they want to fly it on Sunday !!

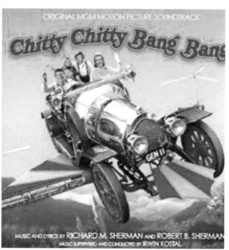

😂👍 John Skelton and 4 others   8 comments

The box and the masterplan.

March 16th, 2020 is a day that everybody remembers, as that was the day that the United Kingdom went into lockdown! Well, I didn't so I had to google it. But nobody will forget the toilet roll panic buying or the fact that people thought that the world was going to end.

I had just returned from my parents' house in Dunfermline, Scotland where I couldn't figure out why they had so many toilet rolls. I would just like to point out that they didn't take all of them, but they could have been involved in the conspiracy!

Let me tell you a little bit about my background first before I talk to you about all the fantastic stuff that myself and my amazing daughters did during the Lockdown.

My name is Rod and I was born in Scotland and I am a single parent of three daughters. Just wait for the audiobook of this you won't understand a word I say.

I live in a one-bedroom flat just around the corner from my ex-wife (who shares the parenting). If there is one thing that I am thankful for, it is that no matter our differences when it comes to the children, we will always be there for them, and I thank her for that.

When we heard that the nation was going to go into lockdown, we worried about how we were going to cope with the children. As you were aware there were so many mixed messages. Most divorced parents did not know where we stood with our children, but we decided straight away that we would be there for them. I received a phone call from my ex-wife who said that I should move back in with the girls as they would miss me terribly during the lockdown.

I finished my work and went straight to my flat and packed everything that I needed and headed to her house. One hour later I was back at the flat. We both decided that there was no way I was moving back in and that we would just handle everything as it comes.

A week before lockdown I acquired a huge cardboard box from my work, and I thought to myself

"I can make a puppet theatre with this box?"

I had always wanted to be a Blue Peter presenter but failing that I always wanted to be a hands-on dad. I didn't want to be a parent who switched on an Ipad or a TV and just sits on their phone all day seeing who loved them on, Facebook. So, I put this box in the back of the Ghostbusters car (that's what the kids call it), drove to my flat dropped it off and picked up the girls from their mums and we went upstairs.

"Can we watch Chitty Chitty Bang Bang? "asked my eldest daughter Heather.

"Ok but I've got something for…."

"Please! "they all said at once

"Ok very well," I replied. We then watched the whole two-hour extravaganza of Dick Van Dyke and co. After it finished, I then went into my tiny bedroom and came out with the cardboard box.

"Right guys, guess what we are going to make out of this?"

"A Chitty Chitty Bang Bang car, "said Heather

"Oh, eh no I was thinking a puppet theatre for the puppets."

"No daddy ''a Chitty Chitty Bang Bang car', said Abbey.

"Please…." said Lucy with puppy dog eyes.

How could I say no to those eyes?

"Oh, well a Chitty Chitty Bang Bang car it is then. "

I thought to myself "How are we going to do that then?

Every time I went to work, I was always on the lookout for anything that would help in our quest to build a Chitty Chitty Bang Bang car. When I saw two plastic tubs being thrown out, I was straight in the bin fishing them out.

We bought cheap white paint from B & M and set about painting our car. Even though my girls were 8 and 3 at the time they were dab hands with a paintbrush and they loved getting stuck in.

When I was posting our progress on Facebook it was fantastic to see the great messages that my friends were sending to me. These helped my motivation and kept my mental health in check.

    This photo was taken five days before lockdown. I was running in and out of DIY centres, hobby shops, and basically any budget craft shop stockpiling, paint, paper, brushes, Sellotape, glue guns, glue sticks, and in this case silver gaffer tape.

    The girls helped me cut up the strips and we covered the front of the car to give it that silver shine. Our dream, our Chitty Chitty Bang Bang car began to take shape.

    The girls were so excited and every day they came over and built the car.

    "I can't wait to play in the park with it daddy, "said Lucy

Little did we know, what would happen next…

Well the hs2 of the driving world won't be completed on Sunday . Did one of the 4 wheels 4 circular cardboard pieces glued together with a toilet roll inside put in the middle then painted accordingly. Cardboard surrounded on the lights and painted gold. Heather put my dads chair that he gave me inside the car and they are all fighting over who takes turns sitting in it. Getting there ....

Two days before lockdown and I was beginning to feel like a Formula One mechanic, waiting to change the tyres and get this finished. When I visited my parents, my dad gave me an old chair saying,

"Give it to the bairn's they'll love it."

And they did. As soon as they caught their eyes on it in my bedroom it was pulled out and put in the car. They fought each other each night just to sit in the car and watch the T.V. There was me saying.

"Heather, you can sit in daddy's big chair."

"no daddy it's my turn to sit in Chitty "she demanded

"daddy it's my turn, "said Abbey

"Daddy, you know it's my turn." cried Lucy.

Time for a toilet break.

Rod Wheelwright
14 Mar 2020 · 👥

• • •

One wheel on. Night night.xx

👍 Bob Doig and 8 others   1 Comment · 1 share

👍 Like   💬 Comment   ➤ Share

So, this was the last picture of the Chitty Chitty Bang Bang car. There were nights when I put a torch behind the lights and switched off the room lights to watch T.V. However, that was as far as our beloved car would get to see the light as two days later the nation went into lockdown.

"What are we going to do now daddy? "the girls said.

Well, I did have a few ideas.......

And so did they.

Chapter Two

Lockdown and the road to somewhere

And so, lockdown began, and as I mentioned earlier nobody knew what was happening. I personally thought that it would be over within a month, and to be perfectly honest it was like the blind leading the blind. It reminded me of the episode of Blackadder when he is given a map from Lord Melchett and is told that it is a map of the New World , only for him to open it up and discover that the map is blank.

"If you can fill it in as you go along, it would be much appreciated Blackadder" asks Melchett.

In 2012, six months after our beautiful daughter Heather was born, I had a nervous breakdown and after many consultations through the years I was told that I had a mild form of bipolar called Bipolar Rapid Cycle or as I call it the grand old Duke of York syndrome. When you were up you were up, and when you were down you were down, but when you were only halfway up, you didn't come out for six months! So, when we were told that we had to stay indoors and only go out if it was essential it didn't bother me in the slightest. However, with my job as a key worker working at a pet food company this was not going to be the case.

I remember on the first day of lockdown driving to work with my letter conforming that I was a key worker. It was like a scene from a zombie movie. There were cars parked everywhere, no children running around, no noise no fun.

When I got to the store no one knew what was happening, but because I had worked in queue management at the Millennium Dome, I just made sure our team were making sure that everyone was social distancing in the queue and that we were keeping to the maximum capacity of people being allowed in the store. Most of the customers were fantastic, but you did get the odd few who just didn't care. It reminded me of the disaster movie "The Towering Inferno" where the actor Richard Chamberlain's character tries to get himself and a few others to jump the queue and try to hijack the chair on the pully so they can be saved from the burning building, only for them to be dragged to their deaths as the pully snaps and they fall to the ground. There were a lot of Richard Chamberlains during the pandemic.

To all my distant relatives
out there please stay
distant xx

This Facebook message which was sent on the same day as my first one just summed everything up. I love my family and my friends. Having worked as an entertainer as a world-famous Butlin's redcoat. Most of my friends lived all over Britain and each year, we all met up for a reunion. Unfortunately, this was cancelled till further notice and with all my family living in Scotland I succumbed to the fact that I would not be seeing them. Then as I was divorced and with no immediate family, I knew that the only people I could relate to were my beautiful, funny three daughters.

So, what was going to be our next project?

I didn't have a clue.

However, the girls did, and it related to all the clutter that was in my flat. I have always been a hoarder and I do believe that the day I get laid to rest in my coffin there will be a few bits of rubbish stashed in there. I had only been in my flat for over a year and I was still getting to terms with the fact that I was divorced. I was constantly getting my stuff given back to me and there was just no room. Especially, when you also had a five-foot Chitty Chitty Bang Bang car smack in the middle of the room.

It was then that we came up with the idea for the next project.

Rod Wheelwright
15 Apr 2020 · 👥

Trying to keep your children busy but you don't know what to do during the lockdown ? Well I copied this of a website . Get a roll of masking tape and mark out a road on the carpet . Then get your Peppa pig toys and hey presto your own Peppa pig world in your livingroomm cost £2. Get in there ...hope the girls like it tomorrow on my birthday xx

"Ah! Lucy, Abbey, Heather who has left this on the carpet?" I screamed as I had just stood on a small figurine of Peppa Pig.

"Lucy" said Abbey

"Heather" said Lucy

"Abbey" said Heather

This was the constant blame culture that I faced and still do to this day. No one owning up.

"Daddy it's messy" said Heather "there is no room."

She was right. If I was having them coming over all the time, they needed something to do while here. You couldn't take them to the play park it was closed. You couldn't take them for a bite to eat as everywhere was closed. You couldn't drop them off at their friend's house as it was not allowed. I had to face facts. They were bored and I had to do something fast. I made them dinner for that night then I dropped them off at their mums.

That night I totally gutted the living room. I gave it a total TARDIS jettison experience and any space that I had in the flat was quickly filled with boxed items, well I wasn't going to throw it out, was I? The carpet was totally clear, now what could we do tomorrow? Then I picked up the Peppa Pig character and an idea came into my head.

The next day when I picked up the girls, I asked Zoe if I could borrow all the Peppa Pig characters and accessories.

"Don't lose them." she spoke.

When I got the girls into my flat, they could not believe how clean it was.

"Have we been robbed?" said Heather

"Eh no! Today we are going to make a Peppa Pig village."

"Yes daddy. Let's do it! "cheered Lucy she loved Peppa Pig.

Straight away they were like the little mice from Bagpuss. They helped me put the masking tape all around the carpet and within no time our village was complete. It stayed up for one month then we changed the format into a board game as seen on the next page.

Right setting up a peppa pig carpet board game for the girls tomorrow.

👍 Matt Macaulay and 4 others

👍 Like   💬 Comment   ↪ Share

Lastly, I would like to point out through the months of April and May it was mine and my ex-wife's birthday and we celebrated just with our three girls and like many others we stuck by the rules. We took lateral flow tests every time either of us had to pick up the girls. Remember that Boris we stuck by the rules.

Chapter 3

Facing up to Mummies

Rod Wheelwright
24 May 2020 · 👥

The government don't know if they are Cummings or going..

😀 Robert Maxwell and 4 others   2 comments

👍 Like   💬 Comment   ➤ Share

I would like to point out that this chapter has nothing to do with any arguments with my ex-wife. As I have mentioned previously in this book (although we sometimes don't see eye to eye), we have always made time for our children and continue to be the best mum and dad for them.

This chapter concentrates on our activities during lockdown between May and June 2020. There were two main factors that changed the mindset of people during lockdown. The first was the "Eat Out to Help out" scheme and the second was undoubtedly Dominic Cummings (breaking lockdown rules and driving to Barnard Castle).

Believe you me there were times when I thought to myself that I could go up to Scotland in my car and see my family and friends. However, the thought of coming back and hearing two weeks later that someone dear to me was on a ventilator and fighting for their life because of my stupidity, filled me with dread. It was a stupid move, and he should never have done it. because now people were saying, 'If he can break the rules then why can't I?'.

When I drove to work each morning, I could see that more people were coming out as the traffic was getting busier. Also, the behaviour of customers towards retail staff at work was getting beyond breaking point.

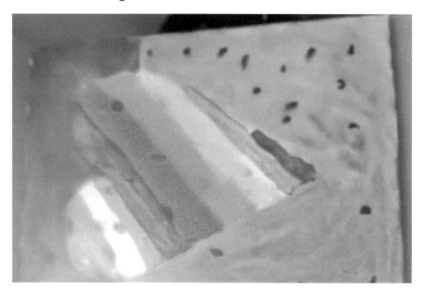
In our store, only two customers from one household were allowed in at a time. Due to the
behaviour of Mr Cummings, people were getting frustrated, and they started taking it out on
the staff.

"You're just a jobsworth'', said one.

"You're just a little Hitler'', said another.

The final straw was…

"Why don't you f..off back to f…ing. Scotland where people can understand you."

This led me to come away from the front door of the store and scurry to the toilets.

My anxiety was going through the roof and all my cognitive therapies (that I had learned)
were all but disappearing. I remember phoning the Samaritans in the middle of the night and
listening to the engaged tone constantly.

 My next activity with the girls would soon put a smile back on my face.

Face Painting

Two baby racoons fast asleep.

 It dawned on me that because of the pandemic no company was doing face painting. So, over the next few months the girls enjoyed getting their face painted. Here is a selection showing their favourite looks.

The witches from Oz

Little rabbitt and spotty dog staying over.

OO Pam Hardman and 5 others   4 comments

Like   Comment   Share

The bunny rabbit and the Dalmatian

Bob Doig and 4 others   23 Views

👍 Like   💬 Comment   ↪ Share

The Tiger Who Came to Tea.

Time to join the hello kitty fan club

The Girl with the Kitty Tattoo.

And of course, there was the mess that was created during all of these activities.

Rod Wheelwright
28 Jun 2020

Daddy: I'm going to just bring a cow into the flat to do a big poo to show you how messy the house is.
Girls : daddy can we ride the cow.

You just can't win can you 😃

Michael Allen

Like   Comment   Share

So now we come back to the title of this chapter 'Facing up to Mummy'. There were times that I dropped them off at their mum's with their face paint still on and unlike the Titanic that did not go down too well. However it was mum that came up with our next assignment during lockdown.

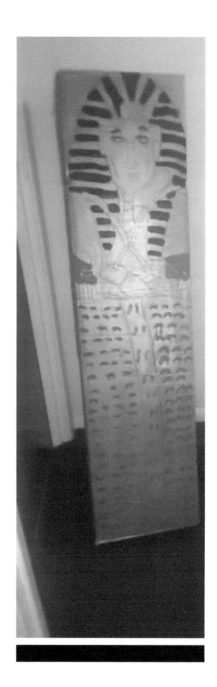

I really felt for my daughter Heather during Lockdown. Although their mum and I were classed as key workers, the school could not accommodate her every day as they were mainly focusing on Emergency Service key workers. So, she only went to school once a week. However, mummy gave us this box shown in the picture and said, "Is there any way you can all make an Egyptian sarcophagus for your class Heather'', as their topic was Egyptian mythology.

So, Heather helped me with the drawing and we masked some of the outlines so the twins could take part too.

The school loved it!

Chapter 4

Normal or Abnormal
Ghostbusting in Gloucester

" Back to life, back to reality." As Soul II Soul once said.

Well, between July and August it did become some kind of normality as restrictions were eased. Masks were still being worn and we are still social distancing. However, as the world-famous R rate was reduced everybody was beginning to come out of their bunkers. This was also when we decided we could take our foot slightly of the pedal so to speak. Also, my humour was beginning to return to me.

 I forgot to mention in this book that before the lockdown I was also running a stand up comedy night at The Dick Whittington in Gloucester and it was becoming very successful. I remember one of my redcoat mates Charlie Damms coming to see me on the first night and later texting me.

" This time next year you will be famous."

Well as soon as I read that text message I am sure I could feel the cold steel of the sword of Damocles bouncing on my neck.

Oh by the way Charlie I am not blaming you for the coronavirus.

Well over the page were just some of the text messages that I was starting to send as my humour mojo was returning.

I made this observation of my girl's

And this comment from a total stranger when we went to McDonald's.

Our feet were firmly of the pedals now and it was time to see what was out there. So, for our first trip we went to Peppa Pig World. We loved it, but there is no such thing as social distancing at a theme park. The staff were fantastic but there is no way you can control that. Luckily, we didn't catch the virus. I always imagine social distancing like fencing. If someone advances towards you then you advance two metres back.

Our second trip was to see an old Butlin's friend of mine and the best clown in the business.

When your stupid old dad forgets to take his mask off for the photo. Ah well at least tweedy the clown is safe.

Ian Campbell and 19 others   1 Comment

Tweedy the Clown

Now if anyone deserves to be famous then it is this guy. The girls absolutely love him. We went to see his show in Cirencester, and it was well organised and socially distanced. Through the pandemic his show was streamed on the internet and the girls didn't miss one performance. Thank you Tweedy for keeping us sane. I would like to point out Tweedy didn't catch the virus after this show. Did you Tweedy?

The last adventure was a solo trip to see my long-time friend Jimmy Griffin in Birmingham. I have known him since we met at Butlin's in North Wales and we always meet up twice a year, so I couldn't miss seeing him. This however was my first ever trip during the pandemic on a train and when I boarded at Gloucester Station it truly was a ghost train. I had the whole carriage to myself. When I met him in our usual haunt at the Square Peg in Birmingham, I could see that the pub was very organised and me and " The geezer " (as I call him) had a brilliant night.

However when I went back on the train home.....

The look I got tonight when I entered the train from Birmingham new street to Gloucester without wearing a mask. Cheers for a great night geezer.

Chris Dawson and 3 others   1 Comment · 1 share

Now this post originally had a picture of Donald Sutherland from the film "The Invasion of the body snatchers" but for copyright reasons I thought I would play out the scene myself.

Now talking about ghosts let's get back to my brilliant girls. They love Ghostbusters and we decided to make some Ghostbusters characters.

Once again I would draw the characters, then let them paint and as you can see below, they loved painting the back packs.

We made a fantastic video which I put on Facebook of us all taking turns playing Slimer or Mr Stay-Puft Man and the girls chasing them in the park. Proud dad not half!

Lastly August 25th is my first-born daughter Heather's birthday and I always feel down the day after her birthday. I think this is because six months after she was born, I had a nervous breakdown. I couldn't cope being a father and having a full-time job and for three weeks of my life I couldn't remember what I'd done. This year it hit me hard and the girls noticed it but then they made something special for me.

A vandalised toilet.

My oldest daughter Heather (who has my sense of humour) got the girls to paint two green cardboard boxes and put graffiti on them. I have never laughed so much in my life. I still don't know till this day where they got this idea from as they have never watched Trainspotting.

Chapter 5

Recreating the Battle of Bannockburn
Will always end in tiers

Rod Wheelwright
18 Sept 2020 · 👥

Hi everyone just to say me and Heather tested
negative for a covid test. Both are back to school/work
today. Thank you for all your kind messages

Love you all

👍❤️ Philip Wheelwright and 38 others   17 comments

👍 Like   💬 Comment   ↪ Share

The Battle with Coronavirus had reached a new turning point in the Wheelwright household
when our eldest Heather was sent home from school because she was showing symptoms of
the virus. This was happening the whole length and breadth of the country because at that
time there were no testing kits. Your child was sent home and any member of that family who
lived with them also had to self-isolate as they may also be carrying the virus.

I remember quite clearly the day before Heather was sent home she stayed over at my flat
and to be honest she was developing a cough but not to the extent that I thought that she
could be infected. I dropped her off at school then went to work. When I got there, I was only
fifteen minutes on the shop floor when I was asked to take a call. It was my ex-wife telling
me the dreaded news. Straight away I told my line manager James and he said, "You'll have
to go home."

Their mum has always worked from home during the pandemic so regardless of who had the
virus she could still work. Luckily our policy at work was that you would get paid the first
time you isolated but after that you did not get paid. I was self-isolating in my old house with
everyone which all the girls loved, however, the next day was a day my daughter did not
love. We had to go to a testing centre to do a coronavirus test.

I will remember this day forever and it is one that every parent will too. Trying to do a test
on your daughter (putting the test stick in your daughters mouth then sticking it up her nose).
The screams were horrific, it was like a scene from The Exorcist. I cried after doing it and
every time from then on. If any of the girls saw me with a test kit they soon scarpered.

The tests both came back negative and as the late Martin Luther King said, "Free at last."

Rod Wheelwright
19 Sept 2020 · 👥

Abbey colours in Rebecca rabbit picture.
What is the grey bit Abbey
?

That is her mask daddy.

Kids eh

This picture which my 3-year-old daughter Abbey coloured in just shows you how much that
the pandemic had affected their lives. It still hangs on my living room wall as a constant
reminder that children never forget.

Rod Wheelwright
4 Oct 2020

Latest news
Dad found starved to death in
Gloucester after 3 daughters eat
all the food

John Skelton and 6 others

One thing they never lost during lockdown was their appetite!

28 Sept 2020

Happy 4th Birthday
To my two beautiful

Lucy   Abbey

Philip Wheelwright and 19 others   10 comments

Like   Comment   Share

The best double act ever had their lockdown birthday.

Trouble in store

So after battles with the virus, it was now time to recreate our own battle. The battle of Bannockburn. The girls were getting bored and there was still no soft play or children's activities out there, so they said to me daddy we want to have a battle in the park. I went to work and took about four huge sections of cardboard home with me.

"Ok guys." I said the next day let's make swords and shields…

18 Oct 2020 · 👥

Going to bed now but tomorrow is medieval night (Knight). So I got some cardboard from work and made these shields and the girls helped me make the swords. Tomorrow when they wake up they are going to paint the rest of the shields and then weather permitting it's a medieval fight in the park.... See more

Rod Wheelwright
18 Oct 2020 · 👥   •••

Funniest thing today was when I was with the girls in the park and we had our battle gear on shield sword and helmets.

I said to heather to close her eyes then I said to my twins to hide in the bushes and when I say charge you have got to come out and help daddy fight off heather

"Ok daddy" say Lucy and Abbey.

The go and hide in the bushes

I tell heather to open her eyes and we both do a sword fight in the park. I then shout Charge.

"IWe need the toilet came the replies from the bushes "

Did William Wallace have this problem at the battle of Falkirk ?

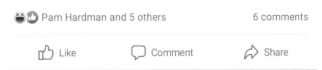

👍 Like   💬 Comment   ➤ Share

Right then girls shields and swords done . Time to make the helmets and invade England.

"Daddy were English."

Daddy "doh ! "

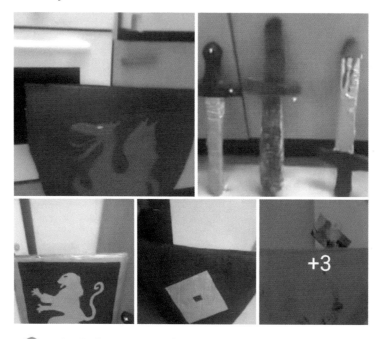

The girls loved making the swords which were made of cardboard but had huge padding of silver gaffer tape. They also added that extra touch of blood on them. They also wanted to have their own personal shield made. Now that is what I call proper warriors.

Abbey defiant !

Lucy "Charge !!"

My bonnie Heather in action.

So, we went to the park near our school and we recreated the battle of Bannockburn. I had my own shield and sword and I instructed them that the only person they can attack is their Scottish daddy.

There were people in the park watching us battle and they were all laughing.
We went for a drink at our local Tesco's and as we were queuing a lady came up to one of the girls and asked where they had got the shields from.

"Our Daddy made them."
"Well done Daddy" said the lady.
The next month we went for a break to Butlin's which luckily did not get cancelled as the R rate (or the oh arrgh rate as they say in the west country) at that moment was low risk. There is one thing you can say about Butlin's, they did a fantastic job during the Pandemic and everything was well organised for our Halloween break. My ex-wife Zoe and I worked and met at Butlin's and it has always been the best holiday camp for family entertainment.
Lastly, I was going to mention my friends Uncle Brian and Jimmy Livingstone getting a Facebook ban, but I don't want Zuckerberg pulling the plug on this do I ?

Sorry Guy's

I would like to point out Uncle Brian was a children's Entertainer and no relation to our family.

Chapter 6

This Christmas our last!
I say not with this farce.
(with help from The Pogues).

I have never understood why people go mad at Christmas time. Six months before the twelfth day of Christmas, someone posts a meme of Will Ferrell and then the riots ensue. When the government announced that there would be a lockdown, the United Kingdom was dragged into chaos (or was it?).

Now, I'm not going into the religious connotations of this, but I thought that our family was going to celebrate Christmas in our bubble. Nothing would make me get dragged into this battle, until this happened.

Well I had to edit that comment as this is a family book.

The greatest Christmas song ever and radio 1 decided to censor these lyrics during a lockdown, were they mad? Well, I was furious. It reminded me of the 80's when Radio 1 banned Relax by Frankie goes to Hollywood (this had the reverse effect) and the song went to number 1. Anyway, apart from that we had a fantastic Christmas.

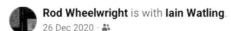

Rod Wheelwright is with **Iain Watling**.
26 Dec 2020 ·

When your young
And your playing with your friends
The days last for ever
The time never ends.
One day you are a soldier
or a pirate on a ship.
Or a cowboy at the ok corral
Shooting from the hip.
Nothing can upset you
Your a hero in the end
Or a bad guy dressed in black next time
You go and meet your friend.
If you hurt yourself your crying
Or screaming going mad
But you can run into that cushion
Called your mum or dad
Then one day you'll grow up
And the playground is no more
The fear when your in action
Or the future you explore.
Just never forget those happy days
Then they will never fade
Sitting in your best friends garden
Drinking fizzy lemonade.

Written by rod wheelwright

Dedicated to my cousin Paul Watling who sadly
passed away.

R.I.P cuz

 Ian Campbell and Iain Watling   1 Comment

I couldn't believe my cousin passed away, so I wrote this poem.

 **Rod Wheelwright**
24 Dec 2020 ·   ...

Daddy.. heather why don't we get the Jumanji board
game. Heather ..it would be too scary .
Daddy.. we are not going to get rhinos coming through
the house..
Heather. Yeah daddy but with your luck.
Daddy.. cluedo it is then

John Skelton and 5 others   3 comments

👍 Like   💬 Comment   ↪ Share

So that was our lockdown Christmas. We spent Christmas Eve at mummy's as always (even after our divorce) and we had a fantastic time. No fuss, no drama, just a family Christmas. We did miss our loved ones, but because the R rate was still high we just couldn't risk it being their last Christmas.

Chapter 7

Back to square one, but we all still had fun.

Happy new year gan yersel !!

As I am writing this chapter, I have just taken a Covid test and for the first time since the pandemic began, I have tested positive. I feel like someone has run me over, got out and checked if I was ok then run me over again. So please be gentle with me.

As you can see by the picture above it was New Year. As everyone was so concerned about getting home for Christmas, this pushed the R rate up again and we were all back in lockdown. Would this be the norm, how long could we endure it?
 Well, it was back to the drawing board with the girls as they needed to be kept entertained. They wanted to do something different. I was making videos on Facebook for the Comedy Club and my daughter Heather said, "Daddy can I make a disaster movie?"

She directed the whole movie entitled "The Flight of Terror ". It revolved around our twins sitting in two car seats and looking forward to going to Peppa Pig World with disastrous results. I added the Psycho music and when we completed it we posted it onto Facebook. During the lockdown we made many videos and hopefully (if this book is successful) I will be able to put them all in an e book.

We also had loads of puppets (which we acquired from charity shops) and we made funny videos of them too. One of my friends Bob, sent me a picture of Big foot and compared it to my current state at the time.

When you just go in the other room for 5 mins peace and your daughter cones in and gives you this.

To daddy please come in we miss you :c

P.s Im thursty

The girls always cheered me up. I remember this one time, they were all arguing and I was trying my best to keep the noise down as the walls in my flat are paper thin. I was always getting complaints from the neighbours. I went into my bedroom for five minutes then Heather came in with this.

It was after this that the girls started coming up with more ideas.

18 Feb 2021 · 👥

It's competition time

👍 Brian Groves and 2 others   45 Views

Play your cards right

15 Feb 2021 · 👥

Pirate ships on hold me hearties due to tantrums but look out for those magnificent ladies in their flying machines xx

👍 John Skelton and 8 others   5 comments · 1 share

👍 Like   💬 Comment   ➤ Share

Flying aeroplanes

Well what a day operation Livingstone is completed and the future of rock and roll is in good hands. A fantastic day had by all I wonder what the challenge is next week.space guns says Lucy....spaceships says abbeyl...TARDIS controls. Got my work cut out there any ideas .....relaxing now and having a can
Love my girls xxx

Kenny Bee and 25 others   5 comments · 1 share

Rock and Roll Legends

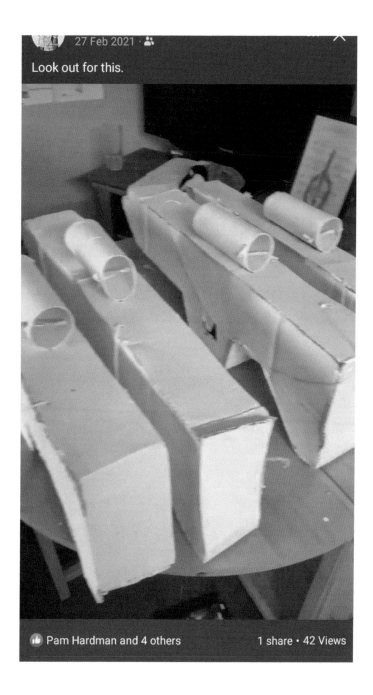

We got out the glue gun and the girls painted these guns white. Then the next day they painted them in their own individual colours. Next, we made a firing range in the living room as you can see on the next page.

The fun fair shooting gallery now taking bookings.

So there you have it our new year lockdown was not shot down in flames.

Chapter 8

Confining with the kids

We were now a full year into the start of the lockdown and both me and my mum and dad
had now had our first vaccination (and at no point when I farted did it send a message to Bill
Gates!).

Things were once again picking up. Then one day when I went to work my Deputy Manager
Jordan said that there was a big cardboard box that I could have (I could turn it into a puppet
theatre for the children).

"That's a fantastic idea" I replied and put the box in my car.

When I went over to pick up the children I said to them that I had a huge cardboard box in the
car and we were going to make something with it.

" What Daddy?" said Heather

" A puppet theatre " I explained.

" Eh no daddy we don't want a puppet theatre. Do we girls ?"

Abbey and Lucy both shook their heads.

" A TARDIS then."

"No Daddy, we want a jail."

"A JAIL ! Girls you don't want that do you ?"

The twins started cheering

They wanted a jail and so we started making one.

11 Apr 2021 · 👥

Can anybody guess what me and the girls are making today ?

👍 Chris Dawson and 3 others   23 comments

We first of all started cutting out the front window for the jail.

More clues what is it

Michael Allen and 1 other   1 share

Like   Comment   Share

The girls set about making it and I posted messages on Facebook to ask if anyone knew what it was.

Painted the jail for them. They absolutely love it. One plays the Gillian one plays the sheriff one plays the visitor and I play the jailer and we all take turns apart from me being the Villian. I can't get in their with my back ..

👍 Pam Hardman and 7 others   7 comments

Now, I should apologise for my spelling mistakes. No one called Gillian was ever in the jail.

Prison life John Skelton

Kenny Bee and 11 others   5 comments · 1 share

The girls have always said that this was the best thing that they made during lockdown. Each of them would basically fight to be the person who was being put in jail. They would sit in there and take turns watching Total Dramarama whilst eating their lunch. It came to the point I had to give them a rota to decide who would be in it !

After our prison adventures we then decided with Mum to have a day release (sorry a break) in Weston Super Mare.

It was just fantastic to see our children enjoying themselves again, they loved every minute of it. At the end of the month we took them to Butlin's Minehead to have even more fun.

Lisa Dawn and 2 others   1 Comment

Then back to real life parenting when I got home.

With the lockdown measures being eased, pubs and clubs began to put entertainment back on and with that the Comedy Club returned. However, it just wasn't the same as before the lockdown. People were still afraid to risk coming out (which was understandable). With growing tensions during the lockdown I just found it harder and harder to write anything funny, and this would play a factor in me deciding to stop doing stand up comedy. So, after two months of having the time of my life with the girls, the next two would be so different.

Chapter 9

It's coming home
But
I'm staying home

Yes it was that time of year, and that sport that all men love was back, football.

Or "Fitba" as it is said in Scotland. This was the first time in over twenty years or so that we had qualified for a major tournament, and nothing was stopping me (a red-blooded Scotsman) from supporting the country of my birth.

Of course, we were not the only nation to qualify. As England or the Auld enemy as we say, were also in the competition.

Now, if any English people are reading this, I am not having a go at your country. I have many English friends, and as you are probably aware my beautiful girls were born in England and are avid England and Scotland fans. They particularly love the England women's football team which we all celebrated when they won the Euro trophy.

I think it's time that they laid the song "It's Coming Home "to rest. Every time there is a major tournament it gets played for usually three and luckily this time four weeks. In this chapter I will explain why it drove me insane.

14 Jun 2021 · 👥

👍😆 You, Richie Welsh and 2 others   1 Comment

👍 Like   💬 Comment   ↗ Share

Well, you never thought that we were going to win the thing, did you?
Imagine that, an Englishman's worst nightmare. I was sent the usual jokes over the internet from my English friends. These include the meme with Spider-Man, as our Scottish goalkeeper David Marshall got trapped in his own net from that goal. I also got sent the usual songs, "You're Going home you're going home. Scotland's going home." And "Scotland get battered everywhere they go."
Well, we certainly didn't get battered in that game, did we?

18 Jun 2021 · 👥

I've promised the girls I'll take them all (including my ex) out for a curry if Scotland win tonight. (heather said it looks like we're eating cat food then !)

😆 Pam Hardman and 4 others   3 comments

👍 Like   💬 Comment   ↗ Share

And that is my bonnie Heather, a woman with sarcasm, a man's worst nightmare.

So, a draw it was. I was so proud of my team. However, five minutes before the game ended I had a phone call from Heather.

"Daddy if it's a draw, do we still get a curry?" she asked.

"I'll tell you after the game'', I quickly answered.

"Daddy, I won't hang up until you tell us we still get a curry if it is a draw'', she demanded.

"Ok if it's a draw you will get a curry'', I said.

The phone went dead, but everyone that night was a winner.

Now, could we possibly defy all odds and qualify for the second round ever in a major final?

People ask with Covid when will life get back together normal. Well Scotland haven't qualified for the next round so we must be .

Like   Comment   Share

And that was basically June and my country was out of the tournament. I was going to mention Matt Hancock's exploits but two humpings in June was enough for me and England had qualified what could possibly go wrong?

9 Jul 2021 ·

Seven days 🥺🥺

I remember the dreaded ping that I got from my phone from Dido Harding's fantastic app, now you know where my Heather gets the sarcasm from. Three days before this everyone went to my farewell party as I was moving to another store. In all four people got pinged that night because we had been in close contact with someone and we had all to self-isolate.

My employers were not impressed, and neither was my ex-wife.

" What do you mean you can't have the girls, it's your day for them'', she screamed.

"I have got to self-isolate for seven days and I cannot have the children'', I replied.

"But what am I going to do about childcare ?"

"I don't know but I can't…"

She hung up.

So this now became the worst seven days of my life. I was stuck indoors with nowhere to go and England were doing fantastic in the Euro's.

Every night I could hear from my window,

"It's coming home, it's coming home."

I genuinely thought that England were going to win it and I was trapped with nowhere to hide.

Well luckily for Scotland they didn't, but for my English friends Charlie Damms, Rob Mcnally, Pete Gallagher and Jimmy Griffin they were coming home, as I was coming out of my Isolation.

10 Jul 2021

Photos sent to me today of abbey Lucy and heather.
Five days to go missing them so much.

Ian Campbell and 11 others   1 share

Missing them whilst I was in isolation.

29 Jul 2021

Bad girls in jail !!

Ian Campbell and 7 others   4 comments

👍 Like   💬 Comment   ↪ Share

The first thing they wanted to play with when I came out of isolation

Chapter 10

Let's pray we never

Have a Lockdown

Again

Currently selling my work uniform on vinted. Making a fortune but a lot of stuff getting nicked at work 😀

😀

Once again, we were drawing nearer to the Autumn and we celebrated into the early evenings our three daughters' birthdays. The world now was beginning to look normal again, as the vaccine was helping with the pandemic. Every key worker had done a fantastic job to keep this country rolling. We however, were still enjoying ourselves.

Beware ! Quicksand !!!

The twins with me and heather on their first trick or treat.

This was our first ever trick or treat with the twins and they absolutely loved it. I played a scarecrow and they dressed up as zombies and a witch. I would knock on the door stand two metres back and stand still like a scarecrow. Then, when the door opened, I would say in my worst Worzel Gummidge voice.

"Hello maybe's you could spare some sweets for these little uns missus."

I can hear Jon Pertwee turning in his grave.

We were out for at least two hours and the girls came back with so many sweets and mum had a well-earned rest.

Our last great work together was this masterpiece..

She loves kitty

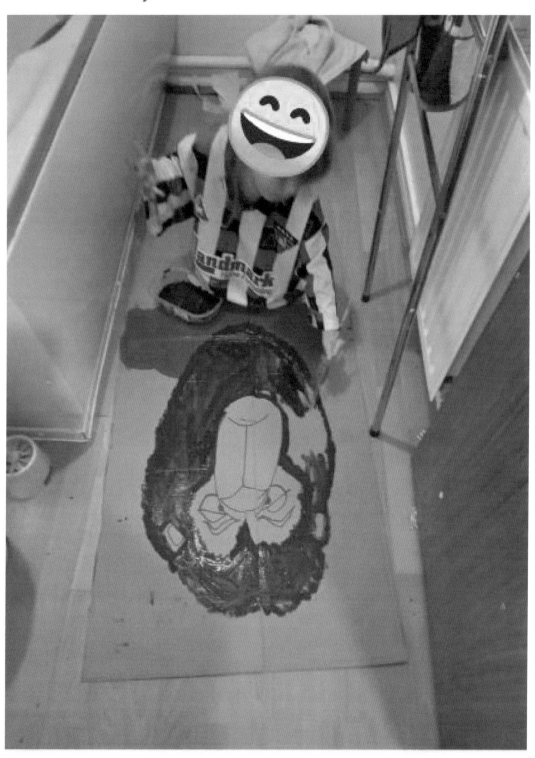

 31 Oct 2021 · 👥

Lurch next lucy

👍 Tracey Coleman and 4 others

They keep my hopes up (🖤🖤

👍💜😄 Pam Hardman and 11 others   3 comments

Our Halloween masterpiece.

The Addams Family

(They are the ones in front)

Heather painted this picture

The Lockdown was over

And here are my three beautiful children in cartoon form. Just like every child they went through tears and laughter. Let us all pray that we are never put in that situation again.

Remember to love your children as they are your future.

Afterword

My Mum and Dad

As I mentioned at the start of this book I had just visited my Mum and Dad before lockdown. All the way through it I wanted to go up but I just couldn't risk it. Every time I phoned them they just wanted to pop outside and go for a drink in the Legion and see their friends. Dad would just love to sing his Elvis songs. They hardly went out during lockdown and when I saw them in February 2022 their health had deteriorated. They are still alive after celebrating 64 years married and before you say it Boris this photo was taken before the lockdown. This book goes out to all the families who lost their loved ones during the pandemic.

In May 2022 I went up to see all my friends at Craig Tara in Ayr for the Butlin's reunion and I never laughed and enjoyed myself so much. I also remember talking to my former Personnel Manager and now SNP MP Allan Dorrans about having this idea to write this book.

"Make sure you write that book Rod'', he said as he left the reunion.

Well I finally did Allan.

And thank you for giving me that spark to write this book.

Oh and one lady we did celebrate on her special jubilee..

The Queen's Golden Jubilee Celebrations.

We made this carriage and Abbey was the Queen and Lucy was the horse pulling her all the way to the school.

They loved every minute of it and Heather dressed up as a Corgi. A fun day for all and didn't everybody deserve it after what we had all been through.

Printed in Great Britain
by Amazon

85453775R00045